C

SAVING OUR PLANET

CONSERVE IT!

by **Mary Boone**

PEBBLE
a capstone imprint

Pebble Explore is published by Pebble, an imprint of Capstone.
1710 Roe Crest Drive, North Mankato, Minnesota 56003
www.capstonepub.com

**Library of Congress Cataloging-in-Publication Data is available on
the Library of Congress website.**
ISBN 978-1-9771-2583-5 (library binding)
ISBN 978-1-9771-2597-2 (paperback)
ISBN 978-1-9771-2603-0 (ebook pdf)

Summary: Introduces early readers to environmentalist concepts
including energy and water conservation, and what they can do to help
the environment. Features real-life examples of kids who have made a
difference.

Editorial Credits
Emily Raij, editor; Brann Garvey, designer; Svetlana Zhurkin, media
researcher; Katy LaVigne, production specialist

Image Credits
AP Photo: Manish Swarup, 15; Newscom: Reuters/Denis Balibouse,
27; Shutterstock: 3445128471, 4, antoniodiaz, 13, Betty Shelton, 17,
curraheeshutter, 7, g215, cover, HollyHarry, 21, IrinaK, 28, LightField
Studios, 5, Madhourse, 29, Monkey Business Images, 18, 23, oliveromg,
11, Rawpixel, 9, Sergey Novikov, 10, Wor Sang Jun, 20, Yuri Samsonov, 24

All internet sites appearing in back matter were available and accurate
when this book was sent to press.

Printed and bound in the USA.
PA117

TABLE OF CONTENTS

Words in **bold** are in the glossary.

WATER AND ENERGY

You brush your teeth. You take showers. You eat food cooked on a stove. You turn on lights in your bedroom. You use water and **energy** every day.

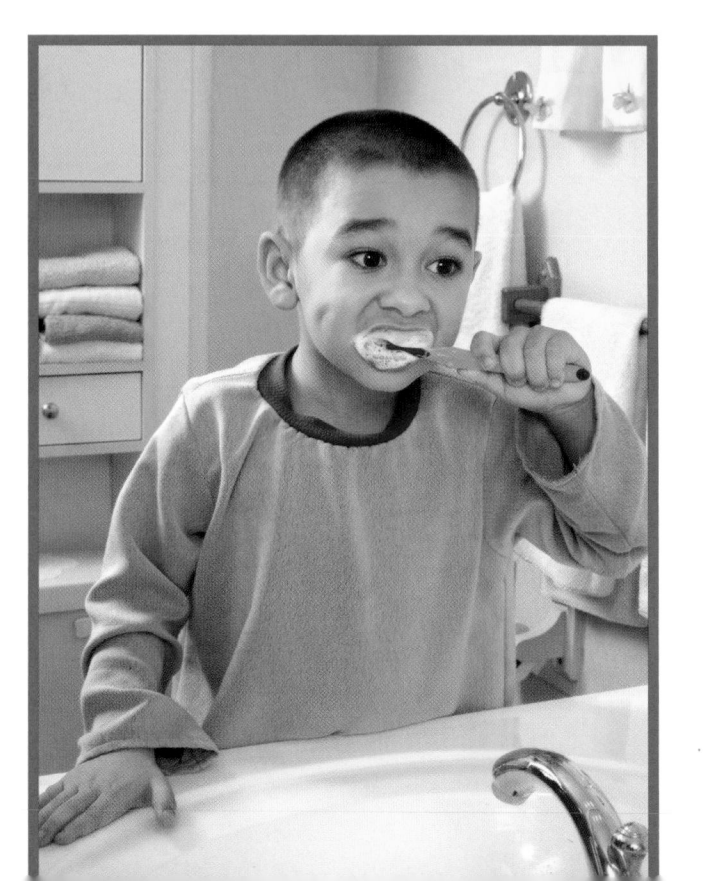

Water and energy make life easy and fun. But their supplies are limited. In order to save our planet, we must learn to **conserve**. That means to save. Conserving water and energy means not using more than you need.

Cars, airplanes, and **factories** use energy. So do things that plug in or use batteries. People use a lot of energy. The number of people in the world is growing. More people will use even more energy.

Some energy is made using oil or coal. Burning oil and coal makes smoke. Smoke can **pollute** the air. Breathing the dirty air is bad for your health. **Drilling** is needed to get oil and coal out of the ground. That can harm the places where animals and people live.

An oil drilling platform

CONSERVING ENERGY

Conserving does not mean using no energy. It means using less. If everyone used less energy, we would need less oil and coal. Our air would be cleaner. We would have more clean water for everybody to use.

Conserving is easy. Adults can do it. Kids can do it. You can do it at home. You can do it at school. Even small changes can make a big difference.

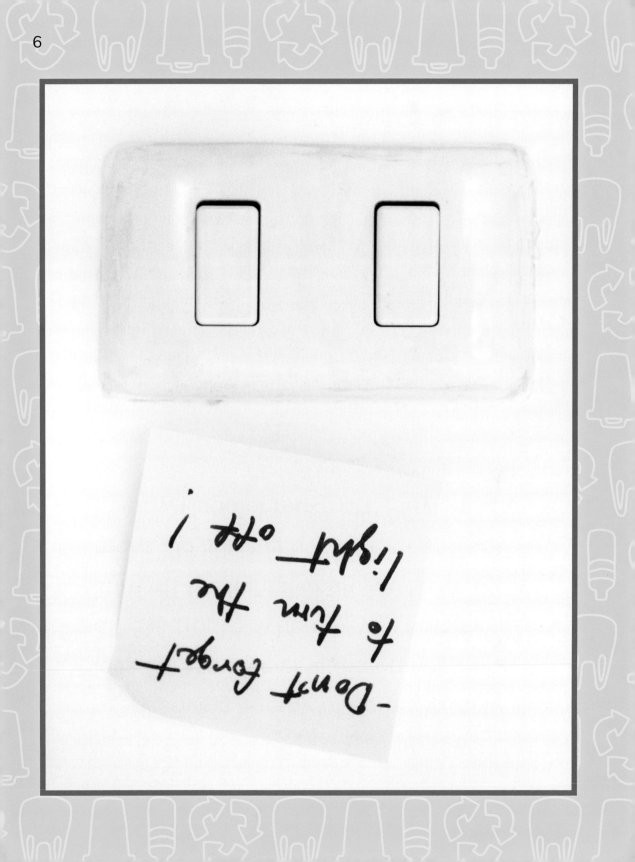

Try saving energy at home. Watch less TV. Play fewer video games. Turn off electronics when they're not in use. Turn off the lights when you leave a room. Do more activities that don't use energy. Read or make art. Play outside.

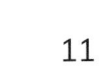

Think about how you go places. Walk to school. Share a ride to sport practices. Take the bus when you can. Fewer cars on the road means less energy being used.

Help your family conserve. Look around your house for ways to save energy. Can you wear a heavy shirt instead of turning up the heat? Does everyone shut the doors when the air conditioner is on? Can you make a meal without **electricity**? Try skipping the stove, oven, and microwave.

Test yourselves. Give a prize to the family member who does the best job of turning off lights.

Ridhima Pandey lives in India. She was 5 when she learned about the problems pollution was causing. She started conserving to help. She taught her friends to save energy.

When she was 9, Ridhima met with her country's leaders. She asked them to make laws about conserving energy. She told them saving energy helps the planet. She is standing up for her beliefs. Ridhima Pandey is a conservation **activist**.

SAVING WATER

Energy is not the only thing you should conserve. Water is limited. Just 1 percent of Earth's water can be used by people. The rest is saltwater or frozen.

Plants, animals, and people need to drink water. Without water, your body stops working. People can only live a few days without it.

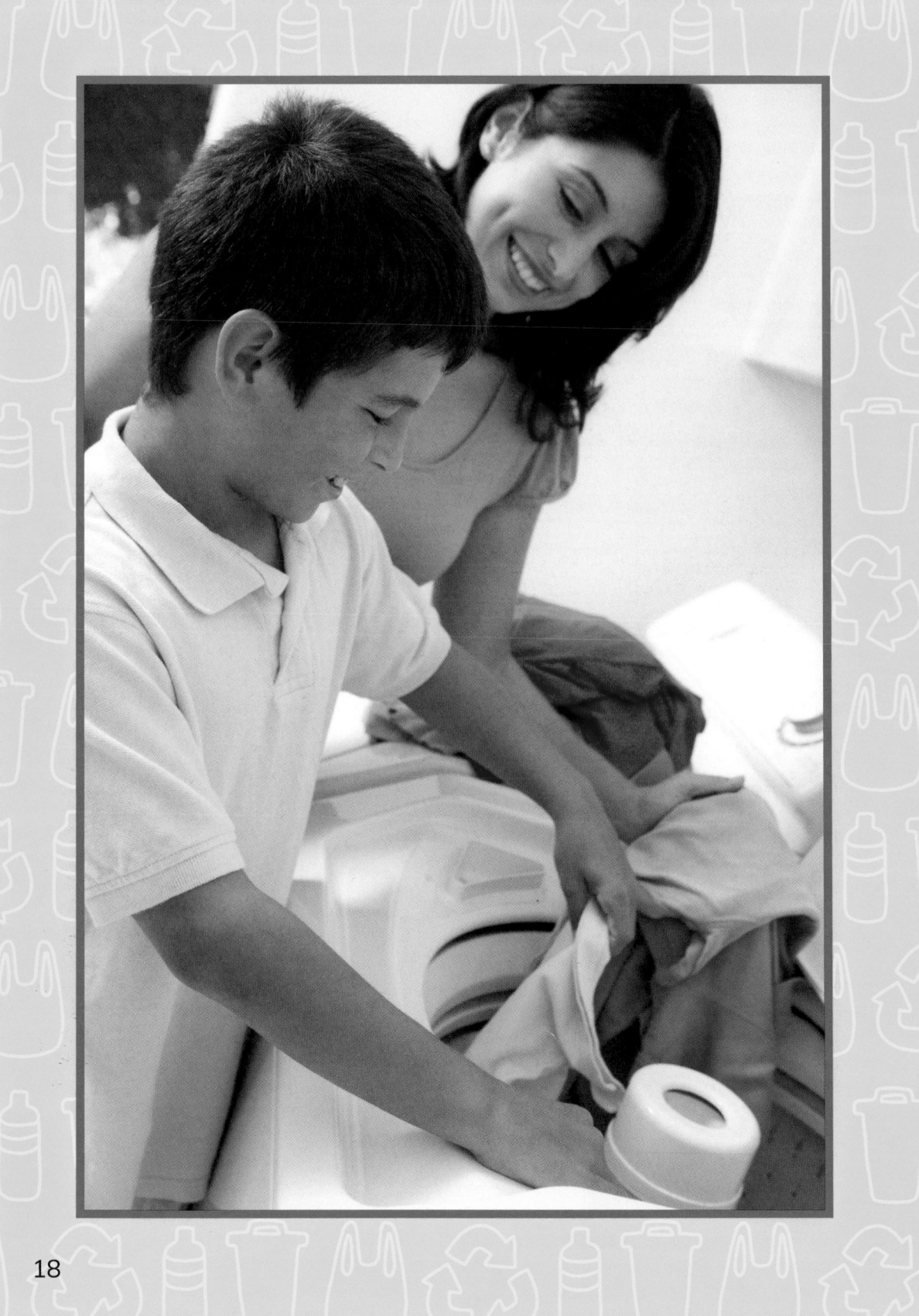

People use water for drinking and cooking. We also use it for washing and cleaning. A U.S. family of four uses about 400 gallons (1,514 liters) of water each day. That's enough to fill 10 bathtubs!

Cities use water to fight fires and clean streets. Businesses and factories use water too. Restaurants need water to cook and wash dishes. Farms use lots of water to grow food. Water is even used to make electricity.

Remember, conserving means not using more than you need. You should still brush your teeth. You should wash your face and hands. But you can save water by turning off the **faucet** while you brush or scrub.

A bath takes twice as much water as a shower. Short showers take less water than long showers. Aim for five minutes or less. Time your shower. Can you shorten it? Each minute cut from your shower saves 2 gallons (7.6 L) of water.

Need more ideas for saving water? Wash your family's car with a bucket and sponge instead of a hose. Collect rainwater for your garden. Dry off with the same towel for several days. Less laundry uses less water. Sweep your driveway instead of spraying it with a hose.

When you give your pet fresh water, don't put the old water down the drain. Use it to water plants.

Get your family to conserve too. Help your parents check for leaky faucets. One drip each second adds up to 5 gallons (18.9 L) per day. That's a lot of wasted water!

Keep a full water pitcher in the refrigerator. Then you won't need to run the faucet to get cold water. Ask about switching to a shower head that saves water. It saves energy needed to heat extra water too.

Autumn Peltier is part of Canada's Wiikwemkoong First Nation. She grew up near Lake Huron. She and her family had clean water. She knows others are not so lucky. Many places have unsafe drinking water.

Autumn began helping to solve this problem when she was 8. Now, she is a teenager. She is still fighting for clean drinking water. Conserving water helps make sure more people get clean water.

27

Earth is our home. People can hurt it. But people can also clean it up and care for it. Learning to conserve helps our planet. Conserving protects the **environment**.

Look for ways you can save energy and water. Flip the light switch off. Turn off the faucet. What other ways can you help?

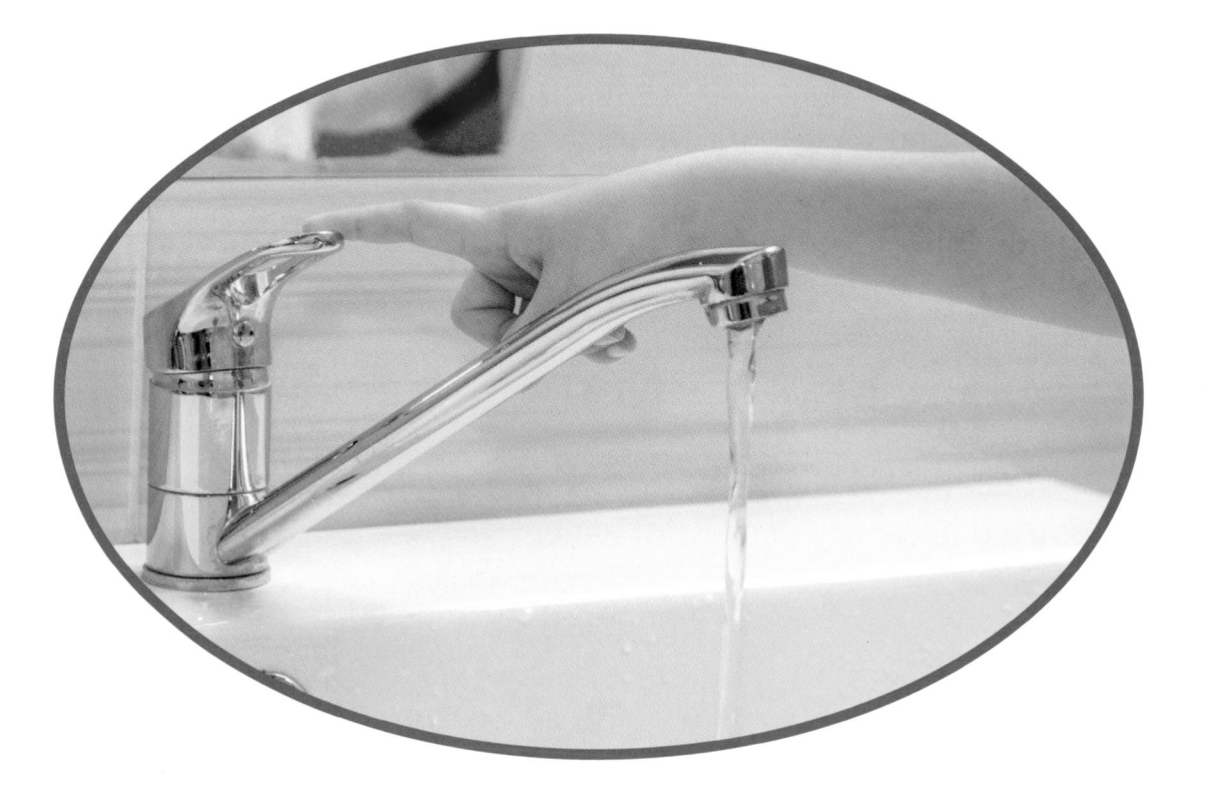

GLOSSARY

activist (AK-tuh-vist)—a person who works for social or political change

conserve (kuhn-SURV)—to save and use in a way that stops something from being wasted or lost

drill (DRIL)—to make a hole

electricity (e-lek-TRI-suh-tee)—a natural force that can be used to make light and heat or to make machines work

energy (EH-nuhr-jee)—usable power that comes from sources such as electricity or heat

environment (in-VY-ruhn-muhnt)—all of the trees, plants, water, and dirt

factory (FAK-tuh-ree)—a building where workers make goods

faucet (FAW-suht)—an object with a valve that is used to control the flow of water

pollute (puh-LOOT)—to make dirty or unsafe

READ MORE

Bullard, Lisa. *Go Green by Saving Energy*. Minneapolis: Lerner Publications, 2018.

Heffernan, Nanette. *Earth Hour: A Lights-Out Event for Our Planet*. Watertown, MA: Charlesbridge, 2020.

Winter, Jeanette. *Our House Is on Fire: Greta Thunberg's Call to Save the Planet*. San Diego: Beach Lane Books, 2019.

INTERNET SITES

Tennessee Valley Authority Kids
www.tvakids.com/index.htm

Water Footprint Calculator
www.watercalculator.org/

Water—Use It Wisely
wateruseitwisely.com/kids/

INDEX